Thoughts and Muses
A book of poetry

.

Sarah J. Waldock

ISBN 1722827882
ISBN-13 978-1722827885

Dedication
To my Dad who taught me appreciation of poetry, and who brought it alive in reading to me. You also gave me my love of words.

Other books by Sarah Waldock

Sarah writes predominantly Regency Romances:

The Brandon Scandals Series
The Hasty Proposal
The Reprobate's Redemption
The Advertised Bride
The Wandering Widow
The Braithwaite Letters
Heiress in Hiding

The Charity School Series
Elinor's Endowment
Ophelia's Opportunity
Abigail's Adventure
Marianne's Misanthrope
Emma's Education/Grace's Gift
Anne's Achievement

One off Regencies
Vanities and Vexations [Jane Austen sequel]
Cousin Prudence [Jane Austen sequel]
Friends and Fortunes
None so Blind
The Unwilling Viscount
Belles and Bucks [short stories]

The Georgian Gambles series
The Valiant Viscount [formerly The Pugilist Peer]
Ace of Schemes

Other
William Price and the 'Thrush', naval adventure and Jane Austen tribute
100 years of Cat Days: 365 anecdotes

Sarah also writes historical mysteries

Regency period 'Jane, Bow Street Consultant 'series, a Jane Austen tribute
Death of a Fop
Jane and the Bow Street Runner [3 novellas]
Jane and the Opera Dancer
Jane and the Christmas Masquerades [2 novellas]
Jane and the Hidden Hoard
Jane and the Burning Question [short stories]
Jane and the Sins of Society

'Felicia and Robin' series set in the Renaissance
Poison for a Poison Tongue
The Mary Rose Mystery
Died True Blue
Frauds, Fools and Fairies
The Bishop of Brangling
The Hazard Chase
Heretics, Hatreds and Histories
The Midsummer Mysteries
The Colour of Murder
Falsehood most Foul
The Monkshithe Mysteries

Children's stories
    Tabitha Tabs the Farm kitten
    A School for Ordinary Princesses [sequel to Frances Hodgson Burnett's 'A Little Princess.]

Non-Fiction
    Writing Regency Romances by dice
    Thoughts and muses [poetry]

Fantasy
    Falconburg Divided [book 1 of the Falconburg brothers series]
    Falconburg Rising [book 2 of the Falconburg brothers series, WIP]
    Falconburg Ascendant [book 3 of the Falconburg brothers series, WIP]

Scarlet Pimpernel spinoffs
    The Redemption of Chauvelin

Sarah Waldock grew up in Suffolk and still resides there, in charge of a husband, and under the ownership of sundry cats. All Sarah's cats are rescue cats and many of them have special needs. They like to help her write and may be found engaging in such helpful pastimes as turning the screen display upside-down, or typing random messages in kittycode into her computer.

Sarah claims to be an artist who writes. Her degree is in art, and she got her best marks writing essays for it. She writes largely historical novels, in order to retain some hold on sanity in an increasingly insane world. There are some writers who claim to write because they have some control over their fictional worlds, but Sarah admits to being thoroughly bullied by her characters who do their own thing and often refuse to comply with her ideas. It makes life more interesting, and she enjoys the surprises they spring on her. Her characters' surprises are usually less messy [and much less noisy] than the surprises her cats spring.

Sarah has tried most of the crafts and avocations which she mentions in her books, on the principle that it is easier to write about what you know. She does not ride horses, since the Good Lord in his mercy saw fit to invent Gottleib Daimler to save her from that experience; and she has not tried blacksmithing. She would like to wave cheerily at anyone in any security services who wonder about middle aged women who read up about making gunpowder and poisonous plants.

Sarah would like to note that any typos remaining in the text after several betas, an editor and proofreader have been over it are caused by the well-known phenomenon of *cat-induced editing syndrome* from the help engendered by busy little bottoms on the keyboard.

This is her excuse and you are stuck with it.

And yes, there are two more cat bums on the edge of the picture as well as the 4 on her lap/chest

You may find out more about Sarah at her blog site, at:
http://sarahs-history-place.blogspot.co.uk/
Or on Facebook for advance news of writing
https://www.facebook.com/pages/Sarah-J-Waldock-Author/520919511296291

Contents

Fae, myth and legend

Fae hunting

Hark! The horn that hearty blows
And winds in woodland's wandering braes
Brangling bells bedazzle foes
The fae folk frolic, and they daze

Lo! How the lords and ladies glide
Garbed in green and glamoured fair
Jangling jewels and gems beside
Circlets of Silver shine on hair.

Fear the folly, follow the sidhe
Shining, shimmering, shallow, wise;
Leeching life, lost in their geas
Gilded but given gifts of lies.

Wondering, wake from bewitched sleep,
Dazed and dimmed in drear mundane
Damned and defiled, in desperation weep
Time taken, teind to the profane.

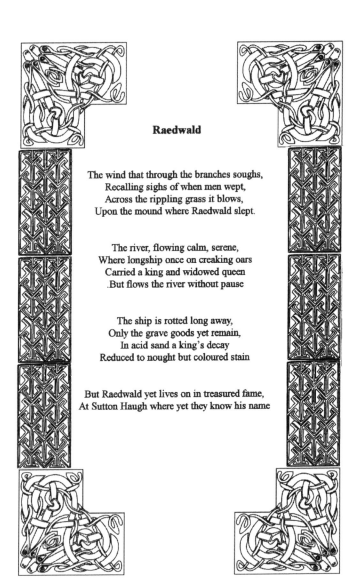

Raedwald

The wind that through the branches soughs,
Recalling sighs of when men wept,
Across the rippling grass it blows,
Upon the mound where Raedwald slept.

The river, flowing calm, serene,
Where longship once on creaking oars
Carried a king and widowed queen
.But flows the river without pause

The ship is rotted long away,
Only the grave goods yet remain,
In acid sand a king's decay
Reduced to nought but coloured stain

But Raedwald yet lives on in treasured fame,
At Sutton Haugh where yet they know his name

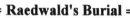

Raedwald's Burial

Sea-skimmer, soil-shrouded
Sea wolf sails in shadow clouded
Portage proudly, prow to stern
Sing the songs the sailors learn.

Heavy the hearts, hauling the ropes
Weeping the women, wailing lost hopes
Carry the king, cauled in his boat
Keening and calling comes from each throat.

Raedwald the ruler, ready and wise
Diplomacy duelled, religion's divides
Symbols of sanctity, signs of the cross
But pagan the prayers of the people's loss

Carry the king as he comes to his rest
Bear the great boat, biggest and best
Soft in the sand under stupendous howe
Raedwald remembered, reliquary now.

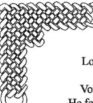

Lonely on the Moor

Lonely on the moor the winds howl
There are voices-
Voices in the wind that chill the soul
He feels the chill; and his blood runs cold

Around a fire three lonely hags
Their vigil keep
These bony crones with clothes in rags
And voices thin as bones whose flesh sags

"All hail Macbeth, of Glamis the Thegn
Thegn of Cawdor
Thegn of Cawdor" they repeat again
"And king thereafter, long may he reign"

Distorted bodies like a starveling child
They dance
They dance, and their contortions wild
Make him feel faint and somehow - defiled

"Till Birnham Wood unto the hill doth come
Then ends thy reign!
Until then, Scotland 'neath your thumb
But beware for it will be your tomb!"

The crackle of the fire; and upward spark
And they are gone
There is no fire, no women: only dark
And dark thoughts of how to make his mark

Lonely on the Moor the winds howl
Nothing stirs
Only the memory of something foul
Only the theft of a human soul....

The Raven

Upon the stump of blasted oak
From raucous throat, the raven's croak
In sombre vigil keenly peers
As have his kin across the years

When Arthur and his peerless knights
Rode forth on quest or hunt or fight
The raven watched in hopes of feast
On fallen man or hunted beast.

And in those days when Merlin strode
O'er tumbled hills or trampled road,
What magic laid on eldritch croak
To tell him how the raven spoke!

Magic passed; but men still waged
The bloody wars that ever raged.
Carrion plenty fed them still,
The sable watchers on the hill

The times have turned; 'tis now absurd
For superstitions round a bird.
But still the raven vigil keeps
While Arthur, 'neath the mountain, sleeps

Old Forest

Come, mortal, come and play
Come and play with us today
We won't let you go away
If you come with us to play

In and out the dappled trees
Sheltered from the sun and breeze
There the fey-folk take their ease
When they come to play

The roads may pass through realms of fey
And all is peaceful in the day
Mortals, 'ware if you should stray,
When they come to play.

For when they come to claim their own
A king upon the seelie throne
The roads shall all be overgrown
When they come to play.

S

A ballad

As I walked home to Ely's Isle
I saw a lady there
With sunken een
And kirtle green
And tangles in her hair.

"Oh do not go by Farsee Fen
There's worse things to be told
Than fenny lights
On darkling nights
Things that would steal your soul."

"I must go home by Farsee Fen
I fear no pixie lights
I'll not be led
I'll hold my tread
And I'll be home this night."

"Then listen to my own true tale
And listen to it well,
For by that way
I went one day
And thus I'm bound for Hell.

"I heeded not the fenny lights
I stayed upon the way,
And in the fog
I heard a dog
That howled a mournful bay.

"And with the dog there was a man
So tall and fine and fair
Still was I held
By his gaze fell
And could not move from there.

"And then he took my frozen hands
And gave me kisses three
'here's one for life
And two for strife
And to steal your soul is three.'

"And now I'm bound to haunt the marsh
But on the soul I lost
My tale of woe
To those who'd go
To save their souls such cost."

Perhaps the woman was deranged
Yet her words I did heed
I stayed within
A merry inn
Until 'twas day indeed.

Runemage

Egil Skalagrimsson took
The poisoned chalice from his host
His smile scarce seen, a thread, a ghost;
The traitor fixed with piercing look.

Manners might yet be forsook,
Defiance to the traitor host
The cup with runes he scratched, engross'd
To neutralise the poison's hook

His hand was firm; it never shook
He did not gloat, he did not boast
He smiled again upon his host
As his own blood he swiftly took

The blood flowed like a sanguine brook
He drained the cup with poison dosed
And called upon another toast
The coward fled, in fear he shook.

Tintagel

About Tintagel's rocky granite shore
Beats the sea in timeless waves that kiss
The rocks in gentle breeze; or wildly roar
As storm winds make the waters pour
And through the wave-cut platforms hiss
While building waves rise more and more.

Here born the heir to lead his folk to war
Arthur, the king, who took the sword as his
Who to his court of Camelot to draw
Those of renown, grim bravery and more
Who saw the Chalice of the King of bliss
Though only one who sought it lacked a flaw.

Merlin connived that this son Ygraine bore
Should be the one who from this act remiss
Grew then to lead his valiant knightly corps
Honour-bound by solemn oath he swore
To lead his folk from barbaric abyss
And give them hope in him for evermore.

And so he sleeps 'til need will him restore.

Nature and Seasons

Sonnet to a skeletal leaf

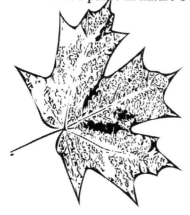

I found one day a maple leaf
Reduced unto a skeleton
So delicate in fine relief
As though 'twere made of Honiton.
I marvel at such beauty, where
The changes wrought by gross decay
Leave nought but delicacy there
With just the leaf veins on display.
Like gossamer, this leafy lace
Needs to be treated with great care
A careless finger out of place
And structure fine is wont to tear.
This beauty made by rot, yet lingers still
Is but a pause in nature's mighty will.

Rain symphony pantoum

Beating, beating on the roof
Raindrops beating like a drum
Pitiless and so aloof
The sharp tattoo an endless thrum

Raindrops beating like a drum
Staccato slash on window pane
The sharp tattoo an endless thrum
The never-ending bitter rain

Staccato slash on window pane
The downpipe gushes forth its flood
The never-ending bitter rain
The ground reduced to seas of mud

The downpipe gushes forth its flood
The water gurgles in the drain
The ground reduced to seas of mud
Under the symphony of rain

The water gurgles in the drain
The sharp tattoo an endless thrum
Under the symphony of rain
Raindrops beat just like a drum

Sea Villanelle

The rolling sea that, restless, plays
Like molten pewter 'neath the sky
Wrought in a plenitude of greys.

Ceaseless the motion, as I gaze,
And listen to the seabirds' cry
The rolling sea that, restless, plays.

Waves beckon to me all my days
Their siren call to me they ply
Wrought in a plenitude of greys

One day I'll follow the sea's ways
And will embrace, with my best try,
The rolling sea that, restless, plays
Wrought in a plenitude of greys.

Frost Smith

Jack the smith's been out tonight
He carved with careful tracery
Each leaf beclad in silver-white
Become a thing of filigree

He carved with careful tracery
Flowers and ferns on windows bright
Like fairy jewels of Gramarye
The mundane made into delight

Flowers and ferns on windows bright
In fractal-formed intricacy
Beyond a mortal's hand or sight
Inhuman in delicacy

In fractal-formed intricacy
Each leaf beclad in silver white
Fashioned from finest fantasy
Jack the smith's been out tonight.

Tree Tunnel

I like to take a walk between
Two rows of trees, that reach and meet,
And traverse through a tunnel green
With soft brown loam beneath my feet

The busy world is far away,
And drowsy bird-song fills my ears,
All troubles fade and have no sway,
Back in proportion, life appears

My heart is filled with tranquil peace,
I smell the green and woody scent
Amongst the tall, eternal trees
Of life and growth 'tis redolent.

And what is time to tall, majestic trees
Its meaning naught to giants such as these

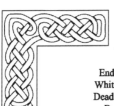

Seasons
inspired by the Kalevala

Endless cold in winter's shiver
White the snow the skies deliver
Dead the world in shroud of icing
But the promise yet enticing
'Neath the frost, the plants lie sleeping
Safe below their blanket sleeping
Frozen waterfalls that capture
Statues of once fluid rapture.

Everywhere the woods are greening
Soft green leaves the thrushes screening
As they sing in springtime fervour
In the newly greening arbour
Joined the song of laughing rills
Chuckling down from off the hills
Icy water melting, falling
Over all, a cuckoo calling.

On the solstice, summer thunder
Slashing lightning, mighty wonder
Then the skies no longer crying,
Sun returns, in splendour drying
Flowers now are all ascendant
Wreathing everywhere resplendent.
Lazy, balmy, cloudless days
Drinking in the solar rays

Swallows leave, migration calling
Brightly coloured leaves are falling
Longer nights and chilly morning
Misty start to autumn dawning
Crackling litter 'neath the trees
Hint of frost in spiteful breeze.
Winds denude the trees at last
Bared to feel the coming blast.

Sunset in metal

The lowering pewter clouds as sinks the sun
Its swift decline, a herald to day's end,
Their heavy aspect leaden, colours run
And leave the sky as day's orb doth descend

Then suddenly! The clouds in shining hue
Of copper, and suffused with light
Unearthly colours as the sun shines through
One last bright challenge to the dark of night.

That light that gilds the buildings, paths and trees
A bronzed and sullen sheen laid over all
A moment's bright caress of sunlight's tease
And then the quiet rain begins to fall.

A steady sheet of silent drops so fine
The bronze glow dragged to earth in gauzy sheets
Puddles like molten metal briefly shine
As though a celestial foundry held the streets.

And then the sky is once more leaden grey
The colours gone and naught but rain and gloom
Even the pewter sheen has gone away
And earth lies under dampened twilight doom.

Poppyfield

When I see a poppy field
(Scarlet stain upon the grass)
I can't resist the sight's appeal
For all too soon the poppies pass.

Silken each crumpled petal red,
As bright a red as may be seen
And sooty stamens in the bed
Against the centre, cool and green

No English field is quite complete
Without its scarlet trim so bold
For poppies speak of summer's heat
And carefree holidays of old.

My favourite weed

Weed, they call you, yet I say
There are few flowers as bright and gay!
Bright in the grass beneath the sun,
A harbinger of spring you run!

Each head a mass of tiny flowers,
Greeting each day's sunlit hours
Like a chrysanthemum writ small,
Growing in lawn, or path, or wall.

Your yellow head is bright to see,
And welcome to the honey bee,
Small beetles in your petals hide
Where they find succour there to bide.

The ring of green leaves round your stem
Are rich food for those who eat them,
And though the gardener they annoy,
I gaze upon you still with joy.

And when your flowering days are past,
Your golden locks grow grey at last,
And rise again with subtle grace,
A globe of winged seeds in place!

Then children puff to tell the time
Which angry gardener thinks a crime
As seeds are scattered far and wide,
All across the countryside

A weed, they say, is just a plant
Growing where others do not want
And yet, I sing a happy paean
To the humble dandelion.

Flying

High up
In the eyrie high
Eagles
Seem to touch the sky

I see them wheel and dive,
In joy to be alive
And flying
I see them wing and soar
I watch in joyful awe
I wish I could see more
They're flying

Up there
In the air so clear
Eagles
From the cliffs so sheer

I see them wheel and dive,
In joy to be alive
And flying
I see then wing and soar
I watch in joyful awe
I wish I could see more
They're flying

Rising
As the thermals lift
Eagles
Through the air they drift

I see them wheel and dive,
In joy to be alive
And flying
I see then wing and soar
I watch in joyful awe
I wish I could see more
They're flying
They're flying
Just flying... ... .

Lonely Hill

I stand upon a lonely hill
In silence but for larks on high
Above the world, I feel a thrill
As down below all scurry by

Below is blue, a misty haze
Concealing all that is mundane
I stand enclosed in dreaming daze
As though exempt from all profane

What changes has this hillock seen
What daily round has slowly changed?
So many lives as there have been
So many bustling things arranged,

And yet the hill in timeless rapture stands alone
To smile derision on our busy mortal bone

Viola

Shy viola that hides her head
Beneath the shade of tall plants lordly
Yet take a closer look instead
And see her regal colours gaudy!

A deeper purple never lay
On royal shoulders velvet-dressed
Nor richer gold could find its way
In human jewellery of the best.

No brocade wove nor damask fine
Could be as finely marked as she
A filigree of guiding line
To help to fetch the passing bee.

And though in modesty she hides
Her finery of royal hue
Her bumbling suitor still abides
Because bee knows her sweetness true.

Spring

The robin sings his trilling song. I hear
The joyful celebrations; it is spring!
The thrush pours out his liquid paean clear
And to the nest with care each twig will bring.

The earth lay sad. Now spears of green
Push up in verdant growth from deep below,
Where bulbs put forth their flowers to be seen
And nodding daffodils; a gaudy show.

Out creeps the frog; from winter's durance stark
He happily resumes his watery home,
His mating song will fill the hours of dark
And frogspawn rises like a jelly dome.

Triple Rainbow

Once I saw a triple rainbow high
The main bow vivid, almost livid-bright
Stretching its colours far across the sky
Encompassing the world with fairy light

Gaudy it stood against the rain clouds grey
But it was not alone! In shadows of
Its glorious hues, one transient ray
Of feeble sunshine showed more bows aloft

Flirting with the sun, around that glorious bow
Above and below, two other pastel-hued
As errant shafts of sun made fickle show
Of arches fair, with magic light imbued

And then I saw the main arch too was more
Its luminescent colours stretched beyond
Purple profound into magenta pure
Reiterating colours so profound

Was this then four bows? I never heard
Of such a thing! I neither know nor care
Enough to have seen it, to have shared
In sublime beauty. I was there.

Shadow and Mystery

Masks

All the world's a stage
Everyone about each task
They wear their opera mask
Staying on the script's right page

Every day we meet
Others in the rat race
Wearing the requisite face
Faces composed and looking neat

All the words are script
Masking emotions every way
If you unmask then there'll be Hell to pay
The words prepared, well clipped.

Fix your face anew
All the masks are fixed to greet,
Fixed to hide the true conceit,
Fixed to smile false smiles on you

All the world's a lie
The masks smile and play their part
Ready to trample on your heart
It isn't safe to pry.

Houses out of cards

I'm building houses out of cards that are as fragile as my dreams
Part of life's illusions, it is never what it seems
One puff of air disturbs it, however big it's grown
And the whole structure will come crashing down

I'm building castles out of sand but they soon will wash away
The sea will take the sand back when the tide returns each day
Nothing to display for all my efforts on the shore
A smooth damp beach just as it was before.

I'm building pipedreams out of hope, which are a shadow of my mind
Like smoke, they fade and wither, there is nothing there to find
I'm building castles in the air, which are going to blow away
Which goes to prove that dreaming doesn't pay.

Puppetry

Dance, suit-man, dance
Dance in Japan, America and France
Throughout the world it's all the same
Acting out your roles for their hall of fame

Dance, suit-man dance
How they pull the strings to make you prance!
Corporate puppets on corporate strings
They write the words to make the puppets sing

Jig, suit-man, jig
But however hard you dance you'll not be Mr Big
Mr Big controls each frantic jerk
Of strings that keep on pulling you to work

Break, suit-man break
When there's no dance to dance and no more left to take
Upon the corporate scrapheap, broken limbs
Free at last from the controllers' little whims

CODA

And shadow puppets held with rods behind the scenes
With foolish shadows caring not and what each movement means
Transient images dependant on the light
That give them substance to show up in the night
And only those who hold the strings, control
Your body and your brain; your life; your soul

Running
[an anapaestic villanelle]

Running on turf and over the heather
Feet pounding on through the wind and the rain
Ignoring the storm and ignoring the weather

Only the sound of the drumming shoe leather
Matching the sound of the heart-beat's refrain
Running on turf and over the heather.

Counting each breath and each footstep together
Soaked to the skin on the soggy terrain
Ignoring the storm and ignoring the weather

Exhaustion that threatens, wondering whether
The spirit can force through the red mists of pain
Running on turf and over the heather

Faltering feet, too much altogether!
Through slashing sleet and hurricane
Ignoring the storm and ignoring the weather

How soon does one reach the end of one's tether?
When will the body's strength then be drained?
Running on turf and over the heather
Ignoring the storm and ignoring the weather.

Turning

Turning from the first pale light
Turning hours until the dark night
Seeking for a way, a means I may start
To unlock the spell laid on my heart

Turning my thoughts with each tomorrow
Hope for my freedom from the sorrow
Is there a way that joyfulness starts
To unlock the spell laid on my heart?

Turn away through changing seasons
Turn away for all the right reasons
Seeking a way to tear apart
And unlock the spell laid on my heart

CODA

Time is turning, a long time turning
Freedom for my thoughts in my heart I'm yearning
Freedom to think the thoughts that are burning
Let my heart be free...

Travelling Man

This-a-way, that-a-way, are you coming back today?
This-a-way, that-a-way, travelling man

He's just a travelling man, with a pack on his back,
He is travelling on, and he won't look back,
He is travelling on along just one track…
To his doom.

This-a-way, that-a-way, are you coming back today?
This-a-way, that-a-way, travelling man

He's a travelling man, and he will not pause,
His travels are aimless, he seeks no cause,
And he turns his gaze from any open doors
On his way.

This-a-way, that-a-way, are you coming back today?
This-a-way, that-a-way, travelling man

He's a travelling man, that's his only goal,
He is travelling on, and it's his only role,
He is travelling on, 'til he's lost his soul
On the road.

This-a-way, that-a-way, are you coming back today?
This-a-way, that-a-way, travelling man

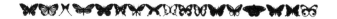

The moth and the flame

Dance like a candle, dance like a flame
Laughing in the breeze, it's all just a game
And after dark when the lights go down.
Just to see those moths come fluttering round.

Pretty little moth all painted and gay
Comes out at night when it's time to play,
She sees the flame that dances bright,
And she can't resist flying into the light.

And the flame dances high and invites her in,
And she quickly flies, with no fear of sin,
Mesmerised by the dark illumed,
And her love consummated by being consumed.

Love

To Simon

I love my love with all my heart
He brings me joy and love sublime
I hate it when we are apart
For any time.

He is my soul's mate, my best friend
With him I can be quite sincere
No masks for him, I don't pretend
When he is here

When hope is low, he lifts me up
Even from the deep despair
His loving smile can fill my cup
Because he cares

Though we grow old with little grace
Though aches are rife in back, knees, hips
I always love to see his face
And kiss his lips

Dancing with you

When the joful music starts
There is nothing but the beat
Keeping rhythm with my heart
And you

My heart beating like a drum
The danceband measure plays
In my ears the blood will hum
At you

Your arms are holding me
I scarcely can feel the floor
And all my eyes can see
Is you

Like eider-down so light
To lift and lightly spin
I could dance this dance all night
With you

Now 'tis you who whirl me round
Faster and faster still
Now I scarcely touch the ground
With you

Tell me O Breeze

Tell me O breeze that softly now doth blow
Have you sweet news from far across the sea
Hast thou, oh Zephyr, kissed my lover's brow
And from that kiss brought tender thoughts to me?

Oh westron wind, didst thou with soft caress
Entwine your gentle breeze in silken hair
Was thy soft breath a kiss of tenderness
Bringst thou love's voice to drive away dull care?

Ah, my tempestuous thoughts in storm-tossed toil
More violent than the blustering of the gale
Long for the breath that kissed my native soil
The gentlest breeze to reach me would avail.

Herein my thoughts a wild maelstrom of yearning need
Await the gentle breath that speaks of love indeed

Love Song for a bard

I played a symphony of bliss
A theme designed upon one tender kiss
I played in a minor key
Because your music cannot be a part of me

I played a melody of joy
The sharps and flats of life may yet destroy
The harmony I play
Because I love too well to run away

I played a carillon of zest
Arpeggios of joy that take no rest
Allegro ma non troppo it must be
For if I go too fast I will surely lose the key

I played a harmony of awe
Each counterpoint to chase the theme and soar
Complex my fugal heart
The end of every song is but the start

I played a serenade of love
The notes I play soar to the sky above
The music that you hear
May yet enchant your heart, entrance your ear

Happy Marriage Recipe

The recipe for happiness, I'm sure you will agree
Contains a pound of silence, if you should disagree
Fling not hasty words in, they will destroy the mix
And leave your well cooked marriage in something of a fix.

But if those words are spoken, before the sun goes down
A handful of 'I'm sorry, dear,' will ease away a frown.
Just bear in mind this warning, and try not to be cursed
By getting in a quarrel over who was sorry first!

Thyme will cure most problems, if enough is then allowed
But beware of too much in the mix, and rising then too proud
And if you feel resentment, then always keep your calm
Season your words when airing it with plenty of good balm.

Rosemary's for remembrance, and remember all that's good
But let bad memories fade away as difficulties should
For bringing up bad tastes again can never be a pleasure
Far better to keep adding spice to multiply your treasure

Miscellaneous

The old coach road

The old coach road cannot be seen
Beneath the metalled tarmac sweep.
You would not know where it had been
Beneath the new road, buried deep.

Where once wound leafy, narrow track
Six lanes of thundering death now steer
Where rumbling wheels, and whip's sharp crack
Were once the loudest sounds to hear.

The cars flash by in ready haste
The coachmen never dreamed such speed!
However fast they may have paced
In rolling coach with foaming steed.

The plexiglass monstrosity
Called 'the old tolbooth' lets us know
That travel did not come for free
And all must pay the pike somehow.

When traffic stills in dead of night
Can you still hear the 'yard of tin'?
The guard's tantivvy blown with might
To warn the gate, or coaching inn.

And through the night in endless cantered pace
The mailcoach runs forever its long race.

Work

Tic! Tin! Tin tan tin!
As he hammers shoe nails in
Cobbler shapes the leather neat
Perfect fit for any feet

Click! Clack! Clickety clack!
Shuttle flies across and back
Weaver weaves a pattern fair
Making cloth for us to wear

Thump! Whack! Thumpity Whack!
Chaff flies, bare the grain to sack
Brawny farmer winnows grain
So we all may eat again

Squmph! Pow! Roll and throw!
Here the baker kneads the dough!
Hot in the ovens bakes the bread
So that we may all be fed

Clang! Tang! Ring bang clong!
Well forged metal sings its song
Braving the heat the metals fuse
Smithing the tools for all to use

Ship of the Fens

Flat lies the land
No hill, no bank, no rise
To break the horizon nothing stands
Just flatness where land meets the skies

The drains cut deep
To drain the marshy fen
And into them the waters seep
Cut to reclaim the land for men.

The mist lies pale
Hiding the rich dark soil
Concealing the farmland hale
Concealing the farmer's toil

A spectre'd mound
Rises from the foggy scene
Suddenly, like floating ground
Revealed where hidden it had been

A ship it seems
That sails the foggy land
Appearing like a shadowed dream
Can this magic too be planned?

Closer one sees
The stonework towers
Buttresses of filigree
Attest to masons' building powers.

Ely Cathedral!
Called ship of the fen
Sailing serene since wrought so tall
Beauteous now as she was then.

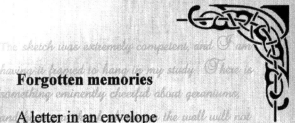

Forgotten memories

A letter in an envelope
Yellow with age, writing aslope
A postcard with a stiff old lady
Labelled simply "Mrs. Brady."

Mementos which were once held dear
Writing strange, and costume queer
Memories now forgotten long
Hints of people weak and strong

Children standing on a beach
Did they for ambitions reach?
Did they live to love and marry
Or did they loveless ever tarry?

Words on a letter to a friend
Precious words to pay to send
Long ago, the question's vexed
What meaning lay within the text …

Mount Rainier

The summit, disembodied, lies
O'er blue and insubstantial shroud
The mountain severed by the cloud
Like magic island fey, that flies

When I see that mountain cone
Incongruously, then I think
Of that joke colour, sky-blue pink
Dawn's roseate hue on snow alone.

And shadows blue reflect the sky
The mountain head defined by light
Soft pastels, magical the sight
And to it then, I long to fly.

Across the Sound, that vision's shine
The magic island in the air
No lower slopes at all are there
The sleeping mountain looks benign.

And yet within is sleeping fire
Volcano's heart of molten death
Which vents a sleeping dragon's breath
Reminder of the dragon's ire.

Sonnet to a scrap of silk

A ragged scrap of silk I find revealed
Brocade of woven flowers in the weft
The greater part of pattern is bereft
How it was finished is concealed.
The flowers gay in blushing rosy hue
As bright as when it came from garment gay
A man's waistcoat perhaps? Or robe Anglais?
Or yet, perhaps, a dainty dancing shoe.
Oh scrap of silk! Did you attend fine balls?
Did you sway in the stateliest gavotte?
Did Madame fan her face, embarrassed, hot?
What scenes did you behold within those halls?
Your story is unknown but my imagination sees
Into the past and the romantic possibilities.

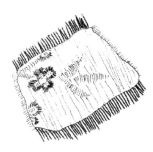

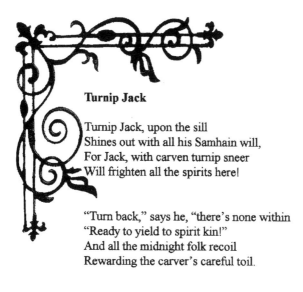

Turnip Jack

Turnip Jack, upon the sill
Shines out with all his Samhain will,
For Jack, with carven turnip sneer
Will frighten all the spirits here!

"Turn back," says he, "there's none within
"Ready to yield to spirit kin!"
And all the midnight folk recoil
Rewarding the carver's careful toil.

And lantern Jack, with candle bold
Frightens the spirit-folk of old,
This day when they are free to haunt
His loathesome face may yet still daunt.

And like the masks that once were worn
His visage guards until the dawn,
When spectres no more may hold sway,
But in the light must melt away.

Fire-raiser Stan

Stan was not a clever boy
At schoolwork he was dire
But one thing Stan knew how to do
Was how to light a fire

He lit them here, he lit them there,
And cared not of folks' ire
For Stan knew he was very good
At how to light a fire.

He burned his mother's bungalow
The flames reached higher and higher
He thought it was a fitting way
His mother to admire

Alas for Stan! No countryman,
To heathland did aspire
To try his hand at setting light
To bracken and to briar

The smoke arose, and crackling flame
And then the gorse caught fire
Farewell, farewell to Stan the man
His massive funeral pyre.

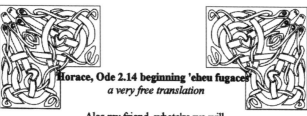

Horace, Ode 2.14 beginning 'eheu fugaces'
a very free translation

Alas my friend, whate're we will
Old age will come and conquer still
No worshipped gods will thus delay
The ravages of time's decay

Not even mighty sacrifice
To tearless Pluto will suffice
We all must cross that gloomy stream
Whate'er our wealth or self esteem

From bloody Mars in vain we flee
And from the waves of the harsh sea
And southern autumn wind whose breath
Is but a harbinger of death

The Lamentation River must
Be faced by those who turn to dust
Passing those damned of Grecian soil
And Sisyphus in endless toil

Leave earth and home and loving wife
Say farewell to all things of life!
Save for sad cypress, trees you tend
Outlive you past your bitter end

Your worthy heir will open wide
Your cellars for what's stored inside
Jealous hoards of wine repose
Imbibed as your bones decompose.

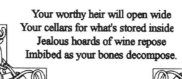

57

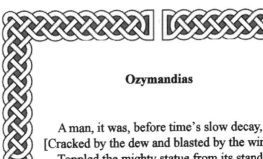

Ozymandias

A man, it was, before time's slow decay,
[Cracked by the dew and blasted by the wind]
Toppled the mighty statue from its stand
Crumbling for the wind to blow away.
The lower half unbroken; yet remained,
Devoid of visage, personality;
Anonymous as a nonentity
Yet on the plinth the statue had been named.
They called him Ozymandias, mighty king,
Rendered in Greek the unfamiliar name,
Certain that all would know of him, his fame
His immortality assured in his standing.

And yet, the writing in his tomb lives on
To tell of Rameses, greatest on the throne

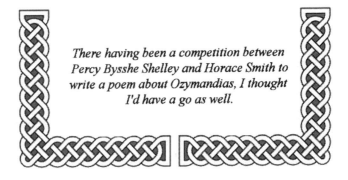

*There having been a competition between
Percy Bysshe Shelley and Horace Smith to
write a poem about Ozymandias, I thought
I'd have a go as well.*

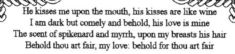

Song of Songs

He kisses me upon the mouth, his kisses are like wine
I am dark but comely and behold, his love is mine
The scent of spikenard and myrrh, upon my breasts his hair
Behold thou art fair, my love: behold for thou art fair

We lay upon a bed of green, within a hall of wood
I am his lily of the valley and I know his love is good
I sat down in his shadow and his fruit was sweet to taste
His left hand is beneath my head, his right doth me embrace

The voice of my beloved coming down the mountainside
He stood before the window as it stood open wide
Rise up my love, my fair one, and come with me away
For winter's past, the rain has gone, and it is fair today

By night upon my bed I sought him, whom my soul doth love
I sought him, but I found him not; so I to look shall rove
I found him and I held him and I would not let him go
I brought him to my father's house to sleep away all woe.

I sleep but my heart waketh for thy voice I hear, my love
Open, my beloved, open up the door my dove
My lover's hand is on the door, my belly stirs within
I open up the door to let my lover come herein

I opened but my lover had withdrawn himself and gone
I went to seek him out but I was frightened and alone
My love was in the garden plucking lilies in the night
He is beautiful and terrible and he is my delight

My love for him as strong as death, it burns with coals of fire
As cruel as the grave my jealousy for his desire
Deep water cannot quench my love, the floods can never drown
Make haste beloved from the mountain, come, my love, come down.

Cats

The old cat, a pantoum

With plodding steps he marches home
The old cat with the gammy leg
Tired from the endless need to roam
Tired by the endless need to beg

The old cat with the gammy leg
Fed at times by those who care
Tired by the endless need to roam
To hope that scraps might still be there

Fed at times by those who care
His efforts take him day by day
To hope that scraps might still be there
Injured, unloved, he makes his way

His efforts take him day by day
Tired from the endless need to roam
Injured, unloved, he makes his way
With plodding steps he marches home.

*Major Tom is his name now; he wasn't that
old and once his leg was amputated and he
got a forever home with us, he never looked
back. Please support rescues like Animal
Action Cyprus, charity number SC046879*

63

Kittenelle

Stalking and pouncing all of the day
Running and chasing the bright butterflies
Great entertainment of kittens at play

One hides in a box and defends it at bay
Without pause, little claws so ineptly he plies
Stalking and pouncing all of the day.

Over the top! There's a tail in the way -
It has to be patted, oh what a surprise!
Great entertainment of kittens at play

Chasing and racing, imagining prey,
Everyone wins for fun is the prize
Stalking and pouncing all of the day

Pouncing spread-eagled, with feet all a-splay
Starfish the toes and great wide kitten eyes
Great entertainment of kittens at play.

A big heap of fur as exhausted they stay
Worn out by their games they are dreaming of mice.
Stalking and pouncing all of the day
Great entertainment of kittens at play!

Kitty Toes

Pouncing, playing kitty feet,
Patting, chasing, seek and hide
Then in joy of play replete
Asleep on back with toes spread wide

Pouncing now, then standing tall
With toes like starfishes, spread apart
Upon his prey prepared to fall
Ready for any game to start

Those wide-spread toes and wide-spread feet
Reflecting his sister's playful pose,
Pat-a-cake gentle paws that meet
So many games for kitty toes.

Rosie

My Rosie reposes
With toes on her nose
She's really quite cosy
In her tangled pose.

Her legs she disposes
In elegant pose
When attitudes dozy
Her sleepy eyes close

And yet she proposes
If she should suppose
A need to be nosy
'Tis time she arose!

Oddments

A few poems which are whimsical in nature, or are poems about poetry like the one below:

Poetry

Iambic is the common form we write,
Two syllables that make up every foot
Unstressed, then stressed, a form that may be trite
But easy then to follow where 'tis put.

Anapaest galloping,
Galloping, travelling
Travelling homeward now
Tired weary Anapaest.
Three simple beats it needs
Here in the anapaest,
Short, short long, makes the beat
Galloping, travelling.

When we use the honest trochee,
Trochee used to tell a story,
Like the song of Hiawatha,
High and mighty is the trochee,
Stressed on second beat is trochee
Stressed to make the rhythm's grandeur
Stressed to show that all is epic
Here displayed before the reader

Villanelle

I like to write a villanelle
Although the form is very tight
It makes my poor head hurt like hell.

I do write other forms as well,
But with this I love to fight
I like to write a villanelle.

With poetry it helps to spell,
And find a rhyme which is just right;
It makes my poor head hurt like hell

Though hard to write enough to sell,
[Poverty, the poet's plight]
I like to write a villanelle.

Is it pretentious? I can't tell
I don't care for that, despite
It makes my poor head hurt like hell.

The poem has me in its spell
It makes my life somewhat more bright
I like to write a villanelle
Although my poor head hurts like hell

Anyone who knows me knows that I love words. I was introduced to the word 'caliginous' meaning 'dark, misty, murky, obscure' and was challenged to put it into a poem.

The Stygian gloom in which they lurk
is caliginous in its murk
And there they hide to bring us shocks
those gremlins who do steal my socks

and

I wake to atramentous gloom
In Stygian darkness shrouded
A truly caliginous doom
The sky, alas, is clouded.

Feel free to write your own, below!

What would a book of poetry be without a few limericks?

Limericks

There once was an old man from Bungay
Who died of a poisonous fungi
They laid him in a tomb
Though there wasn't mush room
For he was far too fat for just one guy

***

There once was a young priest from Bicester[1]
Who got rather involved with a Sister
This nun, from St Mary's
Suffered from caries,
And left the priest's mouth full of blisters.

***

There was an old regent in Brighton
Who said "My pavilion's a right'un
It has domes and arcades,
Pointy bits come in spades
And other such things I delight on!"

---

[1] Pronounced 'Bister'

And finally a few Tanka and Heiku; Tanka have a format of 57577 syllables, and Heiku generally have 575 syllables and are supposed to include a reference to a season, which can be by a semiotic image such as the moon for autumn, or cherry-blossom for spring.

Harvest moon rises:
Golden like the meadow corn.
Gleaming like a coin,
Richly it glows in the sky,
Memory of summer gone.

Slashing rain, spiteful
Biting the face, stinging drops
Soaked through, miserable.

Thoughts crowding my mind
Unruly and disordered
How can I write them?

Autumn moon shining
Early frost, silver filigree
Gleams on fallen leaves

In sunset colours
Bright, though the days are dreary,
Chrysanthemums bloom!

Copper skies heavy
Molten lake reflections gleam
Dark filigree trees!

Thrusting green shafts
Piercing winter's cold mantle
From death is born life

30219627R00049

Printed in Poland
by Amazon Fulfillment
Poland Sp. z o.o., Wrocław